LETTER FROM THE EDITORS

      Without knowing or acknowledging it, you have dressed yourself up in a costume in order to present yourself AS YOU'RE NOT to a world filled with friends, family and strangers. This isn't a call out by any means; we have also been active participants of this age old game. Each and every one of us have a different reason for trying to be someone we're not. It may be because we're hiding our overwhelming sadness from our parents or because taking on a new persona makes our lives easier. Maybe we're simply trying to convince the whole world we are still very much in love with our significant others.

      We have covered our own faces with masks, filters and fake emotions. We have dug ourselves into a hole and thrown out our feelings and identity back up to higher ground. We have all been charmed or forced to believe that showing an edited and cheerful life would be more acceptable and less questioned by our peers.

      Over time, and with much practice, some of us have believed our own lies and deceptions as facts. We start to live deceitful lives that we have so meticulously constructed and the final result can end in two ways: we are either pleased with it and become a better version of ourselves, or our pain and grief continue to rot inside us until we begin to smell the deterioration coming from within ourselves.

      For this month's issue, we focus on these lies and facades without judgment. YOUNG IGNORANTES is a platform that invites you to bring forth this costume and showcase it at every angle. This is the only way for you and us to truly see the heavy mask and come to terms with the reasons why we cover our true selves every single day. We hope that once you read through these pieces and see these glorious displays of creativity that you are able to accept this other version of yourself and embrace it without loathing who you start to see in the mirror. In one way or another, it has become a part of you that really isn't who you are. But in the end, it did come from you some place deep inside. And after you have finished facing this costume and facade, we hope that you begin to show bits and pieces of your true self. It's only appropriate for you to embrace the feelings and the true person that you so tirelessly hide. It doesn't have to be today or tomorrow, but just know that you aren't alone in this game of hiding. Eventually, you have to be okay with being yourself.

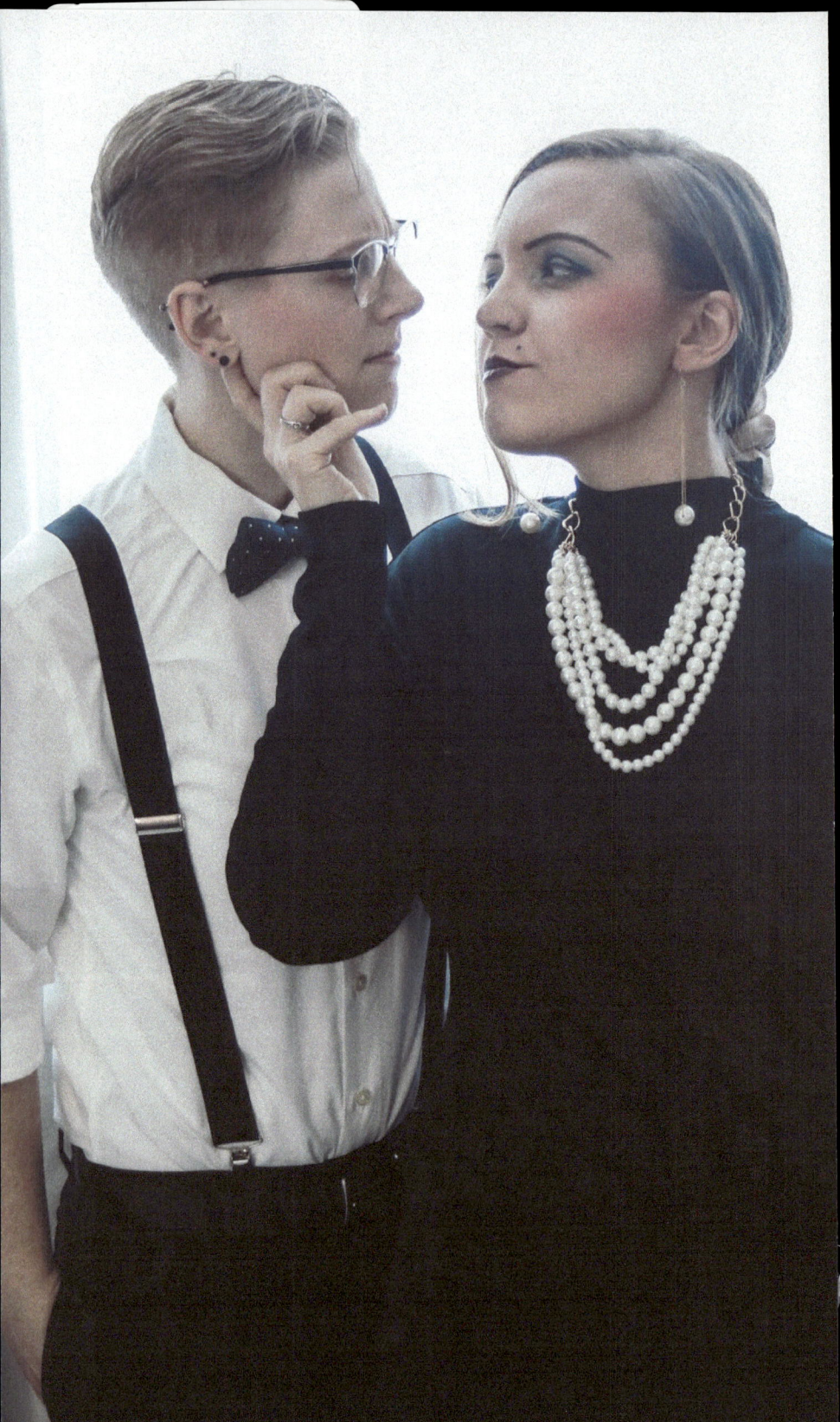

THIS MONTH

- 5 IT FEELS STRANGE TO SMILE
- 7 FACADE
- 10 5-8-17
- 12 INVISIBLE
- 14 NOT A SEED
- 16 SLICED LIFE
- 18 GLOW
- 19 DOUSED IN MUD, SOAKED IN BLEACH
- 20 HOW TO FIND RELIGION
- 28 XXIKKA
- 30 I SEE HER SMILE

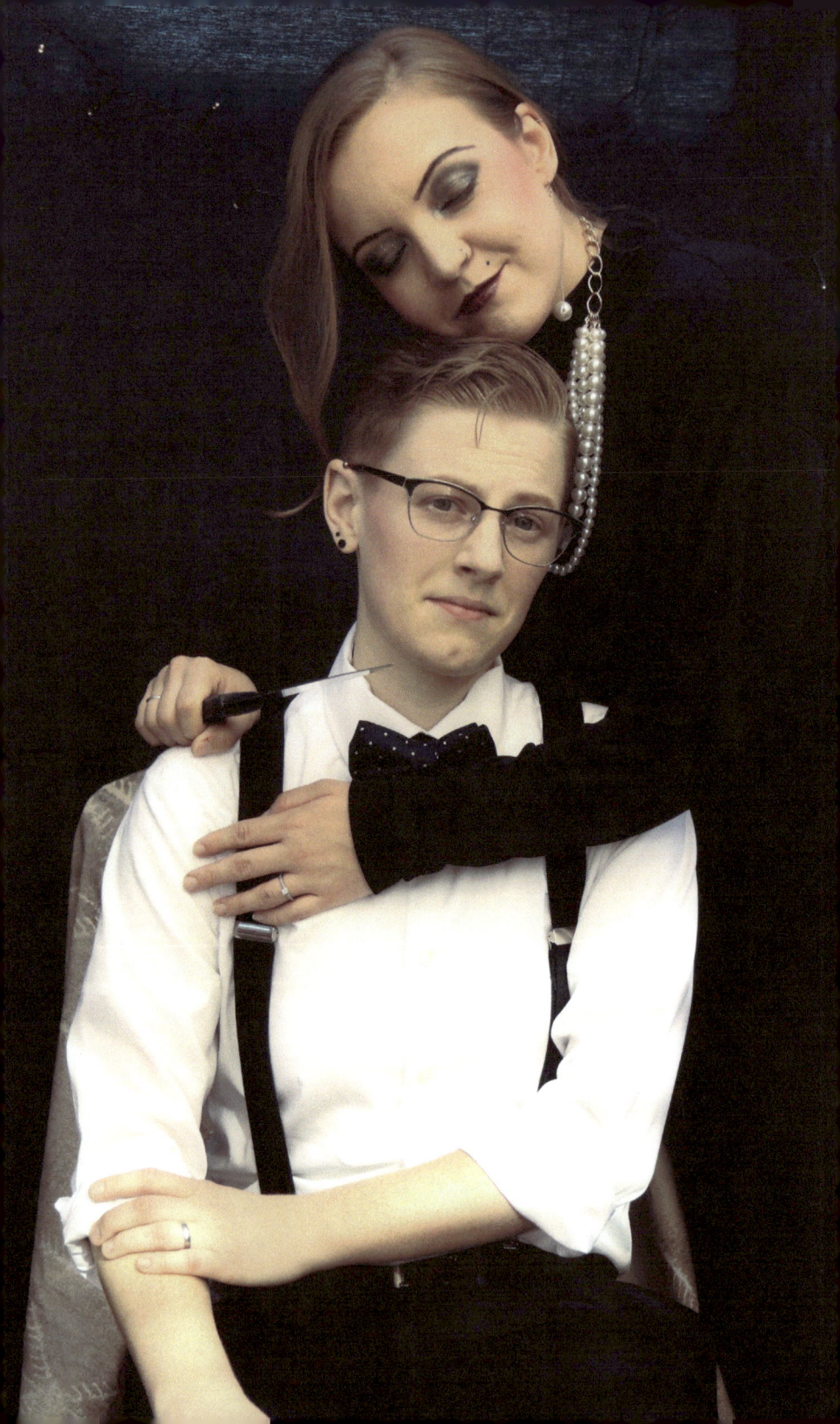

IT FEELS STRANGE TO SMILE

BRENDA HERNÁNDEZ JAIMES

  It feels strange to smile. My cheeks feel heavy when my lips move upwards and my heart stings every time I try to, but if I don't show some semblance of happiness, then people will start to question whether something is wrong, and that's the last thing that I want, the last thing I need.

  Angela has been begging me to take these photos. She says she wants to show the world our undying love for each other, our utter devotion. I had tried to refuse, but she started to question whether I truly loved her. Someone who was truly in love, truly devoted, would have agreed to take these portraits without a second thought. What else could I do but oblige?

  It's too late to incinerate this relationship, to watch it go up in flames. We've been together for too many years now. The fights have become constant and she has repeatedly ripped my heart out and set in on fire, tossing it around like a grenade she's waiting to watch explode.

  She has burned me with her lies too many times. I've lost count now. My friends call me a fool to think that Angela would ever betray me...but I know. The other person always knows. I can feel it in my skin, in every cell of my being. She has a new sparkle in her eye, the same one she had when we had first begun our romance. I've caught moments when she's looking off into space and her cheeks begin to blossom with passion. Deep down, I know she's not thinking of me.

  I'm not the cause of this sudden brush stroke of red across her face. She has found someone else to comfort her, to wrap their arms around her and cover her in kisses full of passion and longing. I've seen her come and go, shining with a beam that blinds me because the light within in her, exuding from her pores. It does not belong to me and it makes me want to sob out of fury.

  I have given her everything...my time, my body, my heart... my life.

  She is my everything, and in turn, she has started to bathe herself in the love she finds in someone's else arms.

  A dark cloud has surrounded us, of that I've been aware for quite a while. I had foolishly believed that she and I would come out of all this stronger, more in love. But it seems she has abandoned me to a new hell, where I watch her fall in love without the respite of knowing with whom or when she would decide that I was no longer worth deceiving.

  I thought that this destructive cycle would have vanished by now, but it seems that this is not the case. The day has been long and I can't seem to take it anymore. What have I done wrong? Did I bring this pain upon myself? Have I not been enough? Has she grown bored of me?

The flash of the camera alerts me and reminds me to play my part. I fear that if I do not become the devoted lover, the ignorant other, then this new love will take Angela away from me. But I can't seem to find the strength to smile anymore.

It's impossible to turn a blind eye for much longer. I've seen visions of them together and now I can't erase them from my mind. I close my eyes, trying in vain to force these thoughts to vanish, but it has been etched into my memory.

It's been too hard to try to bury this betrayal. The smell of a foreign perfume lingers and the sparkle in Angela's eyes enrages my heart.

The only manner to end this battle, this torture, this absolute agony that is taking over my heart is simple, but so unspeakably cruel. The only way to bury this betrayal is to bury Angela. It's the only way take away that sparkle in her eyes.

For the first time in months I feel a smile grace my lips and I can't help but feel hope.

EDITORIAL SHOOT
Models: Catlin Martin & Erika Martin
Photographer: Josephine Jael Jimenez
Stylist: Brenda Hernández Jaimes & Josephine Jael Jimenez
Makeup: Josephine Jael Jimenez

FACADE

JOSE CORDOVA

This hollow feeling, has been growing and eating me from within. In this moment, I wonder how long this will last. When will it end? Yet, every time I step outside, or answer a message, everyone hears, "I'm ok," and I smile.

18 months ago, I sat next to a woman, expressing my love and commitment to her in a way I've never done before. We embraced, reveling in the beauty of that moment of ours. We were smiling.

12 months ago, she pulled away and didn't want to speak to me. Her own confusion and fear of commitment had led her to behave in this hurtful way. My world had fallen apart; my breath grew rapid with my heartbeat. Each day at work, I smiled and said, "I'm ok," while my insides writhed in agony.

8 months ago, I physically withered. The whiskey, insomnia and lack of appetite had changed my appearance significantly. I laid on floors and didn't bother with lights. At work I smiled and said, "I'm ok, its a change in my diet." I began to pray for Death to take me.

6 months ago, we were reunited, much had changed. At first she spoke more and held my hand. We kissed; she invited me to bed. A few weeks went by, the coldness in her eyes and silence of her words returned. I didn't understand why. She disappeared. I reacted. We hurt each other on the phone. She left. And so I smiled and said, "I'm ok," while I was left to hold the shards that were my heart.

1 week ago, she called to apologize and to say someone had hurt her in much the same way. My insides burned. 24 hours ago, she called to say she wanted me in her life but still felt nothing. It felt like torture. I told her to pretend I was dead. For she has destroyed who I was all those months ago. I'll never be the same.

Today, as this abyss consumes me, I know this current life will end. As the love within me dies, I smile at people on the street. When asked, I say "I'm ok."

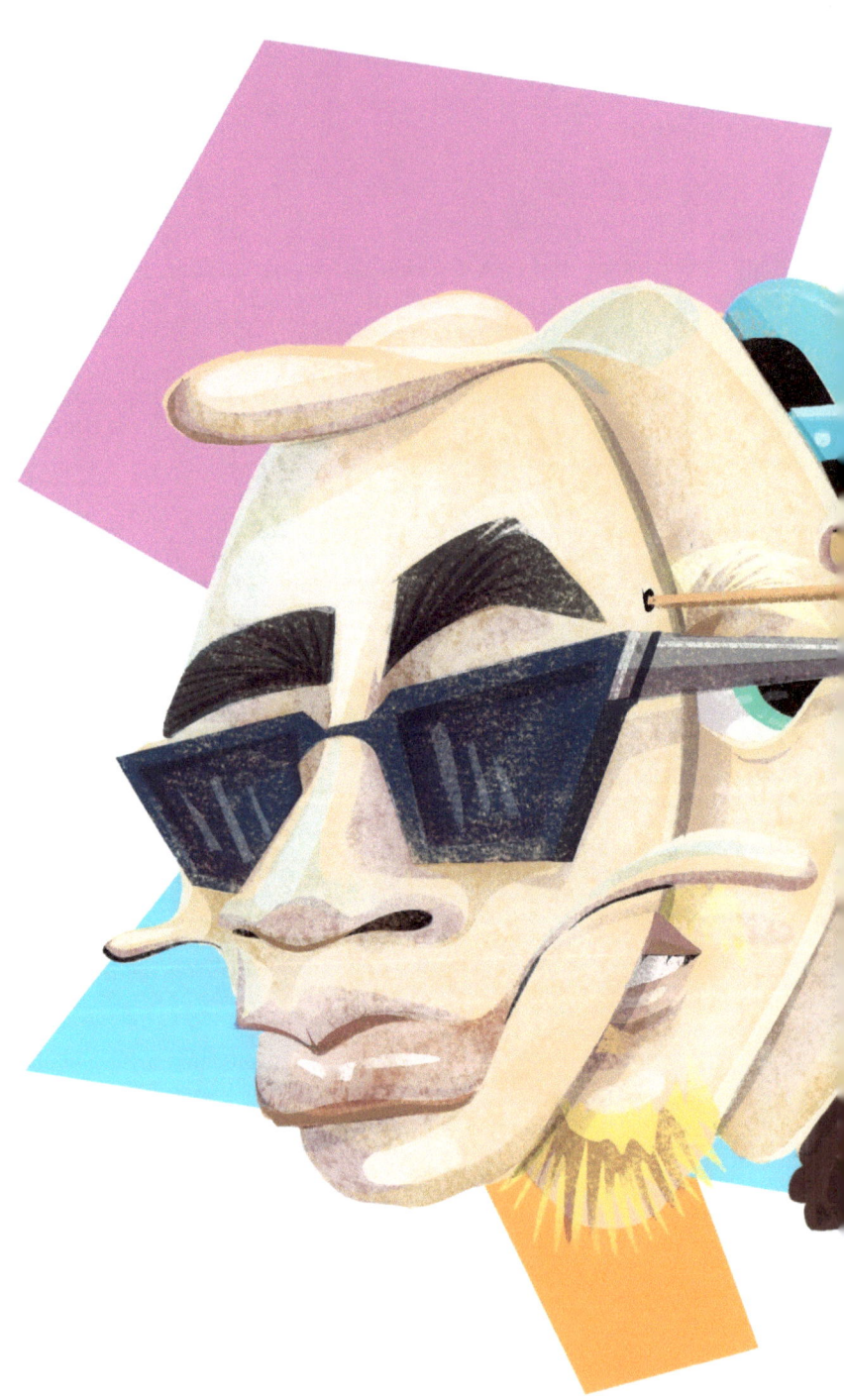

Digital Illustration *by E. Trent Thompson*

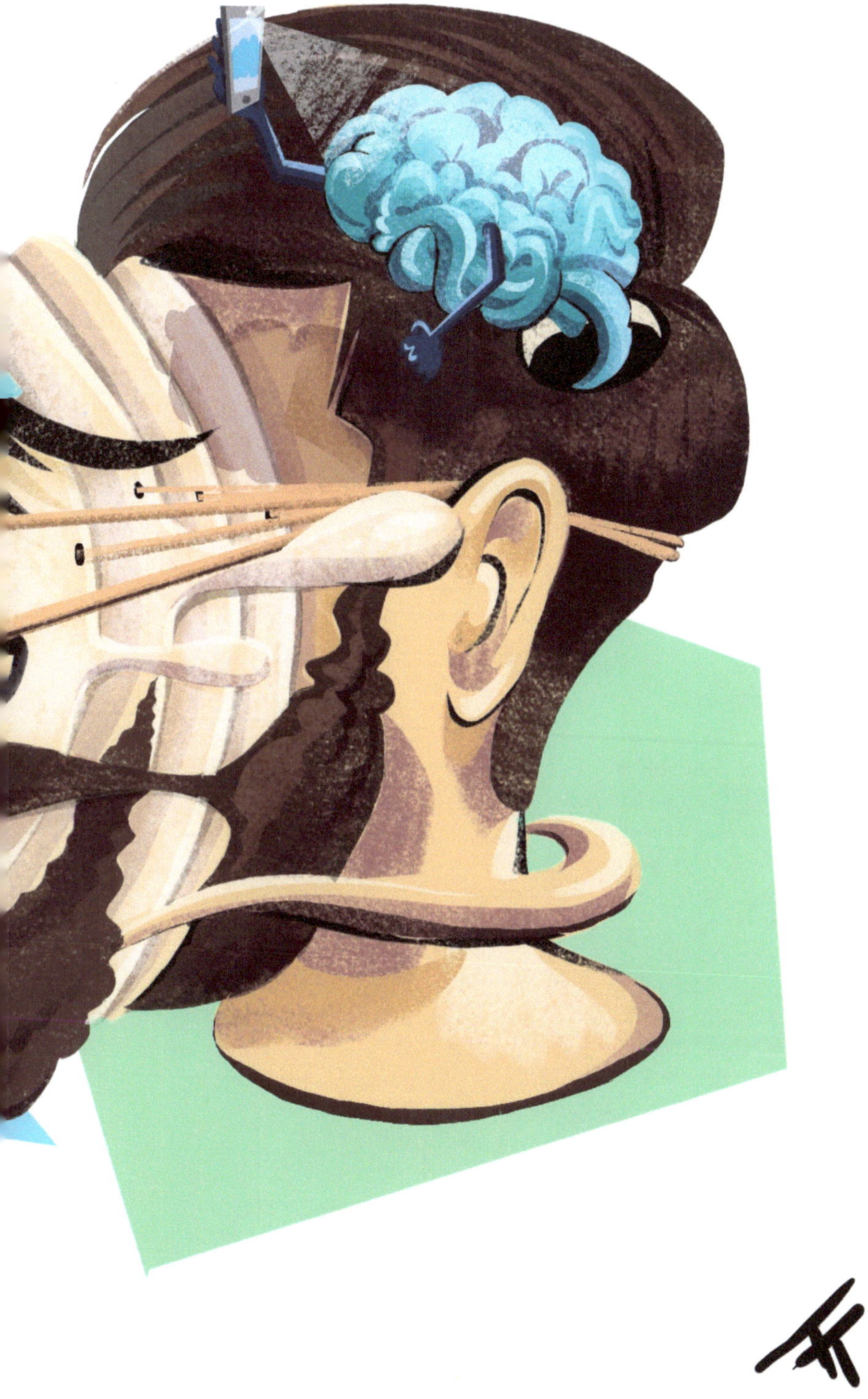

5-8-17

CHELSEA HOYLE

I stir the pot, sinking into a routine. In the next room, my roommate's (possibly ex) boyfriend is asleep on our couch, so I cook by the flashlight of my phone. In the harsh light, I see the fluorescent orange powder still sticking to the sides of the pot. This further cements my suspicions that I am not cut out for a purely domestic life, managing to butcher even a batch of boxed macaroni and cheese. Even so, I mix to the erratic beat of snores echoing from the living room.

"Fine," I had told my mom, only a few hours before.

"Well, that's convincing," my mom replied, her best attempt at sarcasm. She had texted me that morning, asking that I check in with her. Dutiful daughter that I am, I saw the message and promptly fell back asleep.

"Really, it's no big deal. I just need to make the time," I answered, staring at my calendar, days divided and auctioned off to the most pressing jobs.

"The tyranny of the urgent," my mother quipped.

"You could call it that."

I slowly open the cabinet, the door whining as it swings free. What very well could be the last clean bowl in my apartment sits on the top shelf. I scramble to find the footstool in the dark, until I give up and climb on the counter itself. I take the bowl and fill it to the brim with macaroni. Suggested serving sizes are a trap. I glide through my apartment looking for a place to sit, a ghost tripping on displaced furniture and scattered laundry. I fight to put on my oversized sweatshirt and ease open the sliding glass door.

"Good is a relative term," I replied. I was sitting in the library, sunlight flooding through the stained glass display. I had to concentrate on my voice to harmonize with her tone. Kept the notes bright. Didn't slip into a minor or diminished key. My drafts and outlines sat out, increasingly nonsensical, doodles sprawling in the gaps of my research. My friend leaned against the table, legs sprawled into the walkway.

"I guess that's true," she said, her voice breathy but not any quieter. She sighed. I continued to type. I've learned that if someone wants pity, they don't wait for an invitation. "I'm so over this year," she began, "I really don't understand why we have to take Gen. Ed. classes."

"Yeah," I said, while I tried to remember the point I was making in my email to a professor.

"Like, we're never going to use it."

"Sure," I answered, falling into my default responses. I typed my reasoning for why I needed an extension. She rattled on. I thought about finally correcting her understanding of the moniker "liberal arts college," but my laptop was about to die.

"Well, hang in there!" she called after I put my excuse into play. I turned back to return the nicety, but she already found a new captive audience.

  I sit cross-legged on the balcony. In six hours, I'll need to brush my teeth at the very least. I'll skip eyeliner, shaking too much from caffeine or Adderall to pull off a convincing cat-eye. I stir my noodles, steaming in the early morning chill. I should sleep while I can, but I'd rather stay here. I can't even dream that I'm in control.

INVISIBLE

KATIE GARNER

I glance at my arm for the twelfth time. Like the eleven times before, the bulky Omnipod still rests on my arm, tube still piercing flesh. A kind of giddiness bubbles up from seeing it there. The little white box usually sits on my lower back, hidden under my shirt. I brush my fingers over my back's bare flesh, feeling a faint soreness from the needle bruises flowering over my skin.

I carefully pull my bag strap over my shoulder, praying I wouldn't forget the insulin pod throughout the day. Sitting at the kitchen table, Mom sips her vanilla coffee, scanning *The New Yorker*. At the jiggle of my keys, she looks up to wish me a good day before her eye catches the pod clinging to my arm.

She frowns. "Why did you put your pod there?"

"Just wanted to try it out," I say, shoving a sandwich into my bag. "My back is tired."

"It looks weird. It looks like you're proud of it, or something."

My hand freezes on my water bottle. A twisting sensation grips my stomach, and I resume packing.

"What an odd thing to say," I breathe.

I make my way into the garage. Her accusation rocks back and forth in my mind as I turn the Jeep key in the ignition, the engine roaring to life. It seems absurd. But the knot in my gut tightens at the thought.

During elementary school, there was a little girl whose shrunken body and bulbous head drew shocked stares. She couldn't walk. Bones all mismatched and crumbly, she said. Born that way. Nothing to do about it but lots of surgery and a wheelchair. Back then, I thought about how lucky I was, to be born with a broken pancreas rather than a broken body. She couldn't hide her brokenness. Not like I can. Whenever anyone looked at her, the swift and immediate reaction to her bent arms and legs was pity. Who was I to complain about the needles and the headaches and the unquenchable thirst? At least when people looked at me, they saw a person, not a disability.

And yet.

This disease—this thing I've carried with me as far back as I can remember—is a part of me. I don't mean that in the obvious physical aspect, like the needle calluses on my fingers, but in the sense that it has invaded my personality and identity irrevocably. Is it selfish to want that validation? To want people to understand that?

But if I invite these discussions, I must also expect the pity. The awkward explanations. People telling me how "brave" I am. All things part of the package in making visible the invisible. Things I would never tolerate.

After three days, I change my pod. The new one sits to the left of my spine.

NOT A SEED

ELEANOR STELTER

because he said, grief,
all the layers of me were cut back
and the keening was laid bare,
the mourning-bell that's been ringing
for six years. if you listen,
you can hear her name:
Katie, Katie, Katie.
I hold on to her like nothing else
because no one will talk to me about her
without crying. because I'm told
again and again I am so like her,
and I know that I want to be.

that word, grief, it drives its way into me,
to the few things I know, all my own,
and I'm left thinking of chickadees
and my first sip of wine. the way the light
swam in her kitchen in the morning,
the way she talked about art as vital.
beyond these is only the fear,
the knowledge of what happened
next, the slow torture of the months
across which stretched her dying.

misery howls through me, deeper than awareness.
I am a lava tube, burning on the bottom
of the ocean, fire all the way to my core.
there is so much water and so much that
is good between there and here
and a stone where there should be love. I know
my blood will make all things soft in time.
even this, but, Katie, I'm holding on.

LAS MASCARAS Y EL ALMA
Digital Illustration *by Bad Shit*

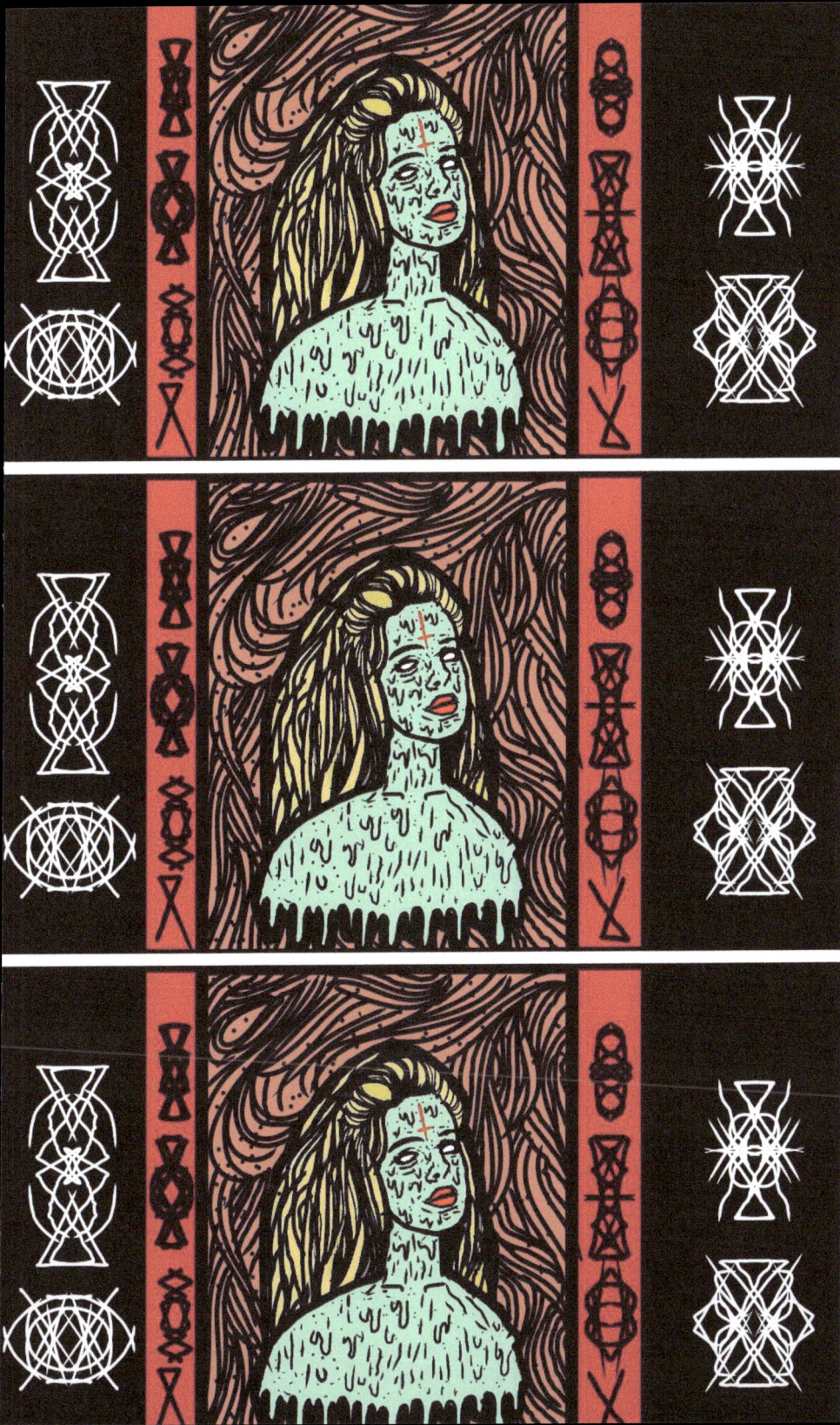

SLICED LIFE

BRENDA HERNÁNDEZ JAIMES

    I've heard all over social media that science says you can trick your brain into thinking you're happy if you just smile. For the past month, while being stuck on the 405, I've been practicing my smile. During this hour and 40 minute drive, I swiftly look at myself in the rearview mirror and flash a big toothy smile that make my cheeks ache because of the weight.

    I didn't realize that I hadn't stopped smiling until my mom made me aware of it and ever since then, I've done this strange ritual of tricking myself into thinking I'm actually happy. However, I find this ritual to be insulting to my brain. I have to give her credit because she's smart, and smiling like a mad woman is not going to make me happy. Nevertheless I've made up my mind, or I've made the decision with my mind and heart, that enough is enough and happiness will once again fill my soul. Even if my smiling ritual is a bit scary to fellow drivers.

    My desperation to slice the dark emotions that threaten to escape my soul on a daily basis has gone as far as to fake smile not only during my drives to work, but in photos that I share on social media. After all, practice makes perfect. But the emptiness that sometimes fills my eyes may be too much for my family and friends and those strangers that like my photos.

    During these photos I don't scare people with my toothy smiles. My smile is small, almost afraid in a way, and I cover my empty eyes with some distracting sunglasses. I can't let people enter the window to my soul, or however that phrase goes. It's too intimate, even on social media.

    I realize that my smiling ritual is bizarre and maybe even pathetic, but in those moments where I am alone, my mind races back to memories of people complimenting me on what a beautiful smile I have. I've never truly believed that compliment. I also remember how last year I felt more happy than I am now. Reminiscing is torture to my ritual and ruins my attempts of feeling and being better.

    Trying to decode the secret to happiness leaves me even more tired and empty than before. My attempts to keep my parents from worrying over me are futile and the wall that I have meticulously built is quickly destroyed by a warm hug. A flood overpowers me and my sad attempt of presenting myself as a strong and happy woman that has her shit together quickly melts away and I'm a toddler once again that is not happy as I've been reminded many, many times before. I'm scared and feel myself drowning.

During this surrender of my so-called strength, I finally realized that the only way for me to once again feel happiness is to let all my dark emotions out and not lock them in. I cannot and will not judge them, I will embrace them in order to let them go and not leave scars in my heart. Maybe once they leave in peace, my brain will finally feel happy and I won't have to fake a smile during my drives and Instagram photos. Most importantly though, I will finally be at peace with myself.

GLOW

MAUREEN E. WOLFF

what does it
take for a
body to glow

light like a
moon over
a world on fire

what name would
you give
me if the fading

was slow
dimming like
lost love

what does it mean
to bloom instead
of cannibalize

and would you
like to know the
syllables that have

lit me up
unhinged in
cosmic brilliance
?

DOUSED IN MUD, SOAKED IN BLEACH

REBEKAH C. GUERRA

A brief reflection on life as carefully orchestrated performance art

---

Do you ever wonder what you could become if you weren't held back by the expectations of others?

I spent four years enmeshed in a culture foreign to me. I constantly changed myself, shape shifting to fit into the mold I was both forced into and somehow also chose for myself. After so many years, it became so hard to tell where the lies ended and the truth began.

It started off as a survival tool and transformed into a lifestyle. For me, it was effortless to go through the motions, to say the right words and build the right relationships. In what was supposed to be a time of self-discovery, I instead spent my time crafting the perfect identity—one that would help me seamlessly navigate my circumstances. I wanted to create a specific impression on others, all as a means to make it out on the other end with my sanity intact.

I had my own forms of protest, the small ways in which I maintained my identity amidst the storm that was my experience as a member of the silenced minority. Sometimes, it was as simple as a particular hairstyle or a new tattoo; other times, it was a seemingly out of place opinion, intentionally stated to plant seeds of subversion in the minds of those around me. I knew I was powerless to make any kind of sustained institutional change, but if I could spur a transformation for a few, then perhaps my great charade was not in vain.

May 6, 2017 was the first day of the rest of my life. That morning, I opened an email from my past self, written two years prior at a particularly low point in what I like to call my "acting career."

You deserve every moment of happiness that you're going to feel today. You're finally free.

2015 me was absolutely right. I am finally free to speak my truth, free from fear of consequences and the harsh judgements of others. Brick and black won't define me forever. I get to make that choice for myself now. I am finally free.

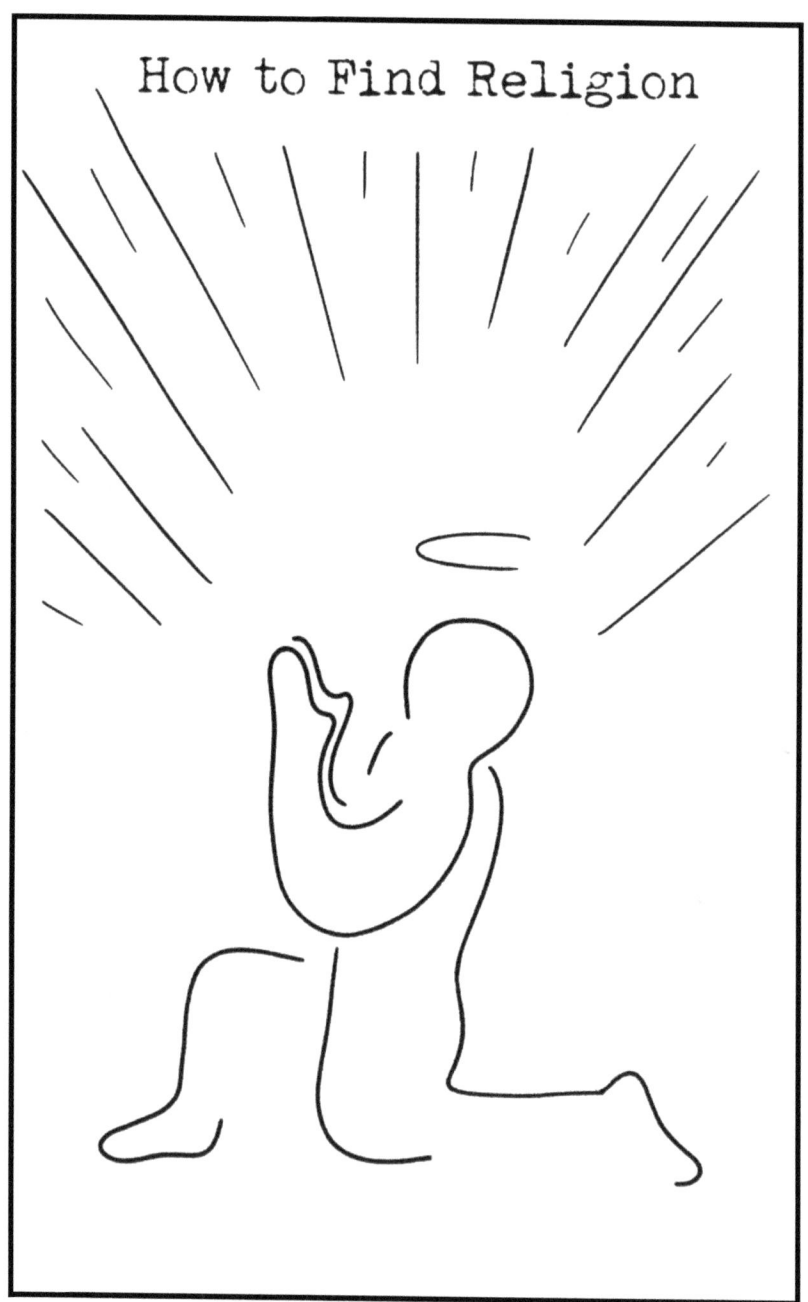

Comic *by Matthew Kramer*

First, yell as loud as you can at the deity that you grew up worshiping.

Yell your grievances & complaints.

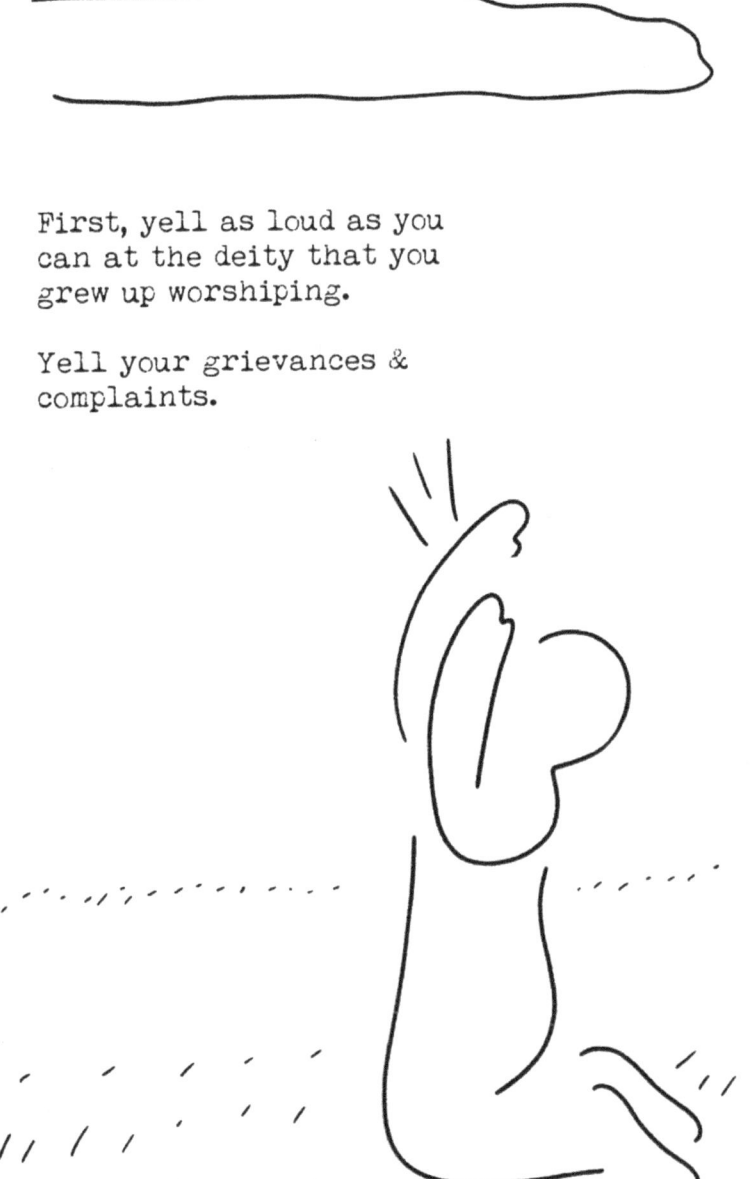

Sit & listen for a response.
They may respond, but few do.
Even if they do, you might not notice.

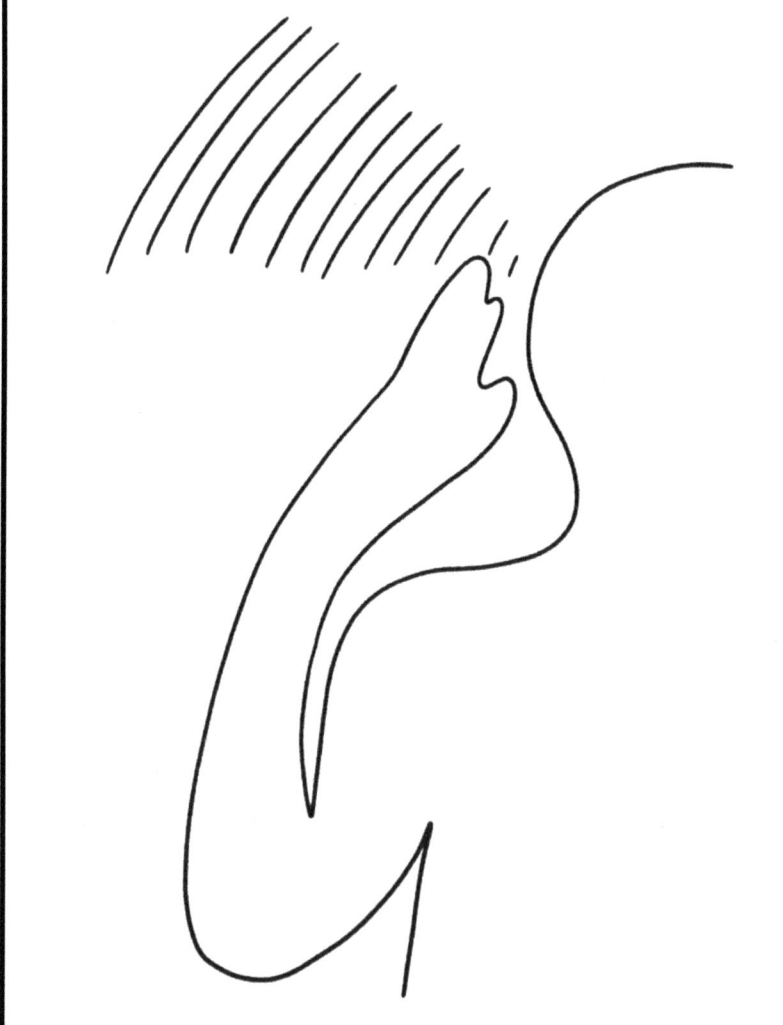

Stand on one foot & think about
your past. Then, jump to the other foot.
As you jump, focus on your present,
& land in your future.

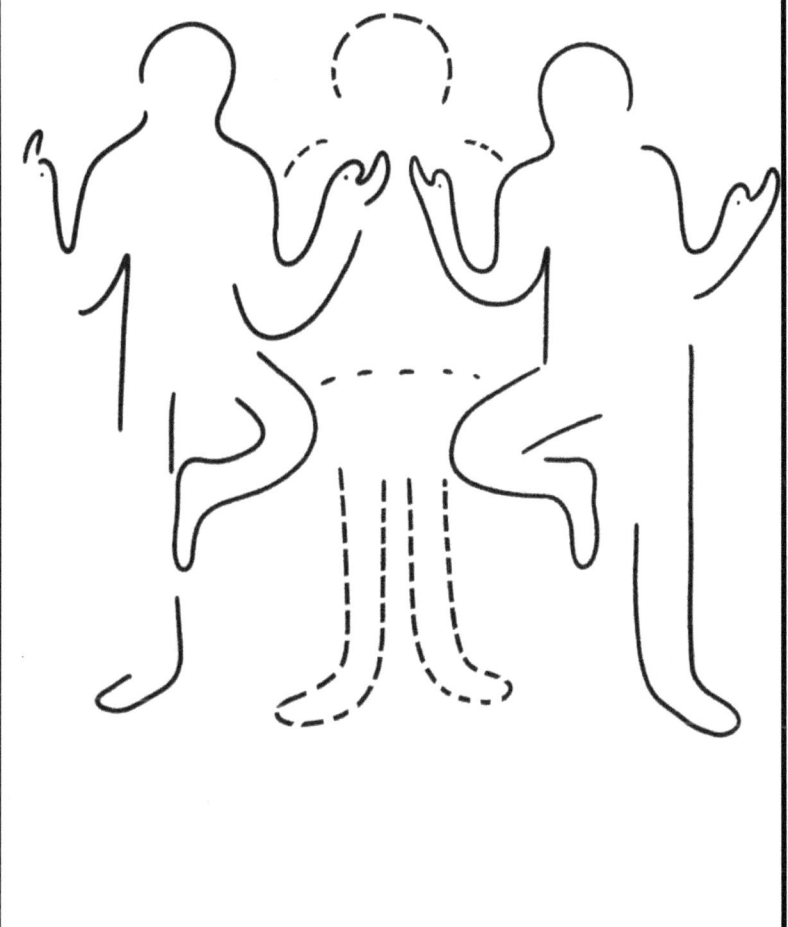

You will have to find your religion &
to do this you will
need an insignificant totem.
Pull an object out of your pocket.
Lint, receipt paper, & buttons are ideal.
If you don't have a pocket, pick
up dirt from the ground.

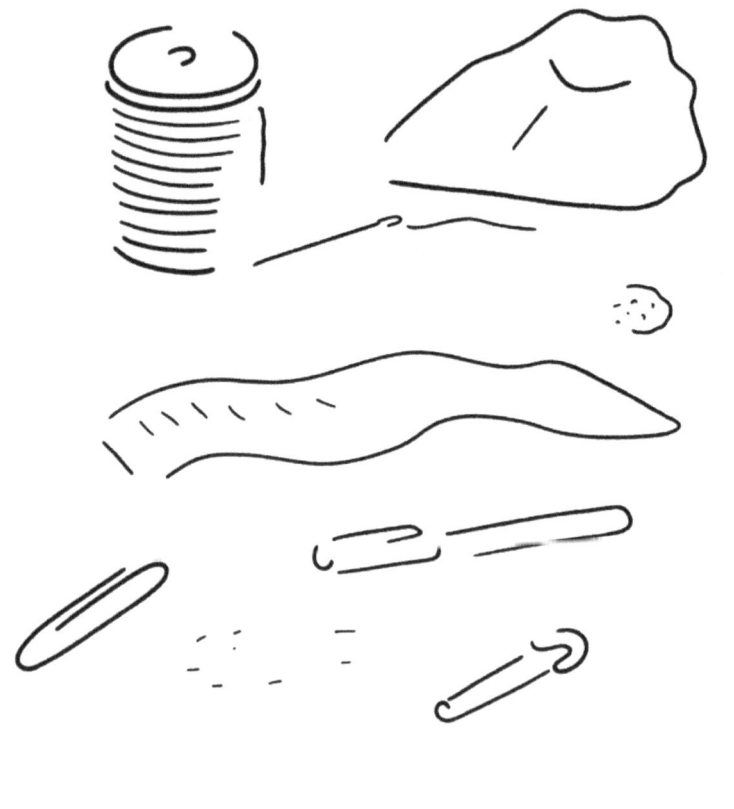

Hold this totem up to the sky & tell your
god what role you want it to play
for you in your life.

You have their attention now.
Tell your god/gods what you need,
when you want it, & how.
Roll dice. If you do not have
die, then use a coin or a shoe.

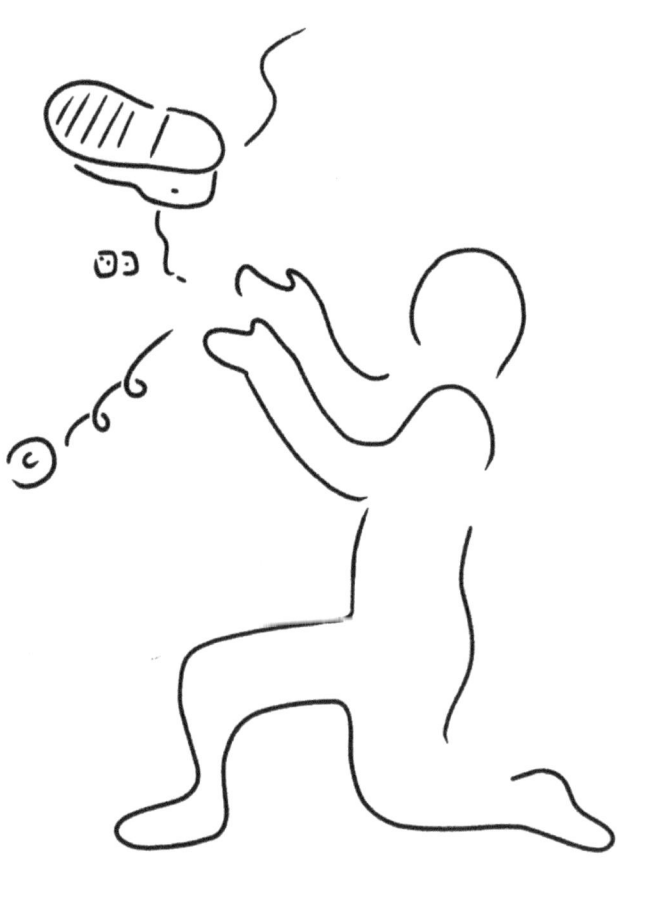

God has now decided how they will help you.
If it was meant to be, it will be so.

XXIKKA

JOSEPH A. REYES

I am the peace within my mother's pain
I am the sensitivity hidden within my father's machismo
I am the escape my nana sought when she left Mexico 44 years ago
I am the manifestation of hope the ancestors called out for when they were
raped
beaten
and assimilated

I am Frida Kahlo
Torn in two
With a heart that achieves in whiteness
But cries out in queer, brown, nonconforming existence

You don't see that
I give you the me you want to see
I give you the me that you see as
Articulate
Docile
Suburban
White

You don't see me as I roll my body to the music that fuels my spirits
You don't see me as I look in the mirror
Naked
Telling my body how beautiful it is
You don't see the scars of the mental and emotional abuse
your culture has fed into my life

You see me as I am, which is as I am not
Truth be told
You don't see me at all
You see the self you've superimposed onto my brown skin
My brown eyes
My dark brown hair
My differently framed body
My queerness

Truth be told
My soul is lighter than your skin
But you can't have that
You never will
Because that's not you

I SEE HER SMILE

JOSEPHINE JAEL JIMENEZ

I'm in love. I'm in love and I undoubtedly care who knows. I sneak out in the day to meet her and I dream all through the night of my sweet angel. She has given me a new reason to live. She is the sun and I am her moon that reflects her light with every step that I take through this cruel world. She is my whole heart, but she cannot be my whole life.

My wonderful wife would die if I left her, she could not survive without me. I am her whole heart, her whole life. But our light has been fading for some time now and I can longer find the joy we once shared. We have settled into a routine that we can't make our way out of. Our lives are too intertwined for me to leave.

We just finished our new fireplace last week. It's lovely and ornate and grand in the way I always hoped it would be. All that it is missing is the portrait above the mantel, the proof of our utter devotion to each other, the cornerstone that everyone can see.

My wife, my Caterina, hesitated at the very mention of the portrait. Part of me worries that she knows, but I have been so careful. She couldn't possibly know. Every other part of me feels heavy at the thought that she may not love me anymore. Does she not love me anymore? I don't know what I would do if that were the case, if she were to become apathetic towards my very existence. I think it would kill me.

But she agrees after some pressure, after another one of our consistent fights. The photographer is hired, the frame purchase, and the clothes laid out on our marriage bed. All is normal, all is well, or at least appears so.

Even as we pose and wait for the photographers flash, I think of my new passion. I can feel her skin, smell her perfume, taste her tongue and I feel my face flush. Surely no one can see, no one will notice.

She's asked me to run away with her, to make a new life in her arms. This is the subject of most of my daydreams, a life where I didn't have to worry about portraits over a mantel or have a wife who is falling out of love with me. A life where Caterina would forgive me for leaving her, where she would understand that time passes and people change, but she hasn't changed. I'm the one who is falling out of love.

The camera flashes and I remember to smile, I ask if I smiled. "No," the photographer tells us. "Neither of you did."

He assured us that it was the traditional way; anyone who is anyone will appreciate our attention to detail, will love the way we stuck the the usual ways, the old ways. It isn't everyday, he says, that marriages last.

For the first time in a long time, I see my wife smile. She looks uncomfortable, out of practice with the way her lips curl upwards. For the first time in weeks, months even, we don't fight. We eat out dinner quietly. I glance up at her time after time to catch her smiling in my direction and it makes me hopeful for the future. She doesn't know. She isn't falling out of love with me. Things will get better. We will love each other, and I will find my passion with someone else. Many a man has held a mistress, why can't I? Who's to say I can't love two people in different ways? My wife doesn't need to know and I don't need to leave the life, the society, I have grown accustomed to. All can be well, all can remain the same. The dreams I hold in my heart of a new life can be enough for me.

We go to bed without a fight and my Caterina holds me in her arms the way she used to when we first fell in love. She holds me tight and I find comfort in her for the first time in years. The smile on her face gives me hope that we can be together forever, like we always promised.

OUR PEOPLE

BAD SHIT
@bad_shit
fb.com/okreskate.rodriguez

BRENDA HERNÁNDEZ JAIMES
@bren_jai
brenjai.com

CAITLIN MARTIN
@caitietastic

CHELSEA HOYLE

E. TRENT THOMPSON
@etrentart_
etrentart.com

ELEANOR STELTER
@moonquistador

ERIKA MARTIN
@erikatellefsen

JOSE CORDOVA
@wrdspektor

JOSEPH A. REYES
@joeykangarooooo

JOSEPHINE JAEL JIMENEZ
@josietakestheworld
josietakestheworld.com

KATIE GARNER
sisyphusrising.tumblr.com

MATTHEW KRAMER
@canttakemeanywhere
matthewckramer.com
canttakemeanywhere.com

MAUREEN E. WOLFF
@maureenwrites

REBEKAH C. GUERRA
rebekahguerra.com

YOUNG IGNORANTES
@youngignorantes
youngignorantes.com

www.ingramcontent.com/pod-product-compliance
Lightning Source LLC
Chambersburg PA
CBHW040342220526
45473CB00009B/2764